HOW TO RAISE A TODDLER

Powerful Strategies for Toddler Parenting, Discipline, Behaviors and Tantrums

JOY LAMAR

COPYRIGHT

DISCLAIMER & STATEMENT OF RIGHTS

This report is for informational purposes only and the author does not accept any responsibilities for any liabilities or damages, real or perceived, resulting from the use of this information.

While all effort has been geared to ensure reliability of the information within, the liability, negligence or misuse or abuse of the operation of any methods, strategies and instructions/ideas contained in the material herein is the sole responsibility of the reader/user.

This material is from the view of the author. It includes information, products, or services by third parties. Third Party materials comprise of the products and opinions expressed by their owners. As such, the authors of this guide do not assume responsibility or liability for any Third Party Material or opinions.

JOY LAMAR

CONTENTS

Introduction

Thank you for grabbing a copy of this book. In it, I will be showing you ways to understand, communicate with and discipline your toddler: ways you've probably never heard before.

Applying my simple suggestions will also help you deal with the terrible twos' poor child behavior and tantrums and all sorts of other parenting problems.

Some of the things you will come across in this book may very well be the most enlightening parenting instructions you've ever heard of. And I believe you'll be amazed.

I have to assume that if you're reading this book, you have probably been dealing with a lot of stress or anxiety that stems from being a parent.

You love your kids so much, yet they sometimes drive you crazy, and their behavior and actions make you worry that you are not doing a good job of raising them.

The good news is that you can get the changes that you want. Experiences have proved you can actually turn things around and really start to enjoy your kids and your time as a parent much more than you are right now.

I'd like to help you to make those changes starting right now by showing you some of the most important tools you can learn.

Here's more good news. Most of the problems you're facing with your child's behavior are not your fault. Think about it. Toddlers don't come with instruction manuals like machines. They are as human as you are, and they are just what you once were.

Also, parents don't get trained by anybody on how to deal with toddlers and preschoolers. They don't teach this stuff in school. You may have taken one of those parenting classes when you were expecting your first child that teaches you how to hold a baby, how to feed a baby and other stuff like that.

Sure it's important stuff, but it's actually pretty easy when compared to practically facing the terrible twos, the horrible threes or perhaps, the freaking fours. These experiences pose big-time stress for parents.

You can learn and apply better ways to deal with your kids by finishing this book.

There are lots of moms and dads who feel like they're failing as parents. I know you want peace and quietness in your home. I have to let you know that you're not alone. In fact, you're in very good company.

The only real reason you don't have the peaceful home that you want, with well-behaved kids is that nobody's ever given you the right information and the proper tools. You've either been given no information, or even worse, the wrong information. Here we are going to fix that. Let's begin.

PART 1:

POSITIVE

PARENTING

What is Positive Parenting?

It might be helpful to consider what positive parenting is not, in order to accurately see what positive parenting is. Think about all the methods of discipline that you're familiar with; spanking, yelling, grounding rules, and timeouts.

These methods are negative in nature because when you adopt these methods, you punish your child for misbehaving. The fear of getting punished again, in the same manner, is what is supposed to prevent your child from misbehaving again.

Even though negative discipline works, it's not a long-term solution. Chances are you're going to be repeating the same motions again very soon.

How Is Positive Discipline Different?

Positive discipline is different as it aims to teach your kids important social and life skills in ways that are both encouraging and respectful, both to the parent and the child. In positive parenting, parents try to figure out the motivation behind a child's misbehavior.

Would you consider yourself a positive parent? Here are some questions you need to ask yourself:

Do you communicate with your toddler in a kind but firm manner?

Does your interaction with him foster respect both to you and the child?

Do you encourage children to be independent and use their abilities in a constructive way?

Do you teach lifelong lessons to your child?

Do you consider your disciplinary measures to be effective in the long term?

If you answered yes to these questions, you're already practicing positive parenting at home with your kids. But here is an opportunity to learn more about positive parenting, please read on.

Always remember, there is no such thing as the perfect parent. But you can always be a great one.

Parenting Styles

There are different techniques parents use to raise their kids. Let's take a quick look at three of them;

1. Authoritarian parenting
2. Permissive parenting, and
3. Positive parenting

Authoritarian Parenting

Let's imagine your toddler attempts to climb on a couch in your home. It is obvious she cannot succeed in that activity, but what does she know? As a parent, you are concerned that she may fall and get hurt in the process. So you go to her and yell, "I have always told you not to climb on anything! Get off that couch now!"

This is how a typical authoritarian parent will react. Makes no attempt to explain or empathize, the next thing he does is remove the child from the couch.

We know toddlers for who they are, especially the stubborn ones. The child may try to climb the chair again and the parent spares no time in removing the child again. Only this time, the kid gets punished by the parent.

Authoritarian parenting gratifies the bossy part of us. But to punish a toddler who might be having a tantrum or bad behavior is not the ideal solution. Punishments cannot teach children the values of good behavior. Nothing disconnects a parent from his child as much as punishment does.

You may think it's good to punish your kid for a bad behavior, but your toddler's little brain cannot process the reason he is being punished. He may not see it from a perspective of hurting himself. All he sees is a dad or mum who does not want him to have a certain experience.

In the same way that toddlers may find it difficult to comprehend why they are being punished, toddlers may also not understand when you explain to them.

However, you develop a positive bond with your child when you try to explain to him that he is being punished in his own interests. And that's a good thing.

Permissive Parenting

At the other end of the spectrum lies permissive parenting.

Faced with the same situation as the authoritarian parent, a permissive parent may say, "What would I do with you Tracy? Mommy says do not climb the couch, it's too high and you will hurt yourself."

And that is all. The parent actually does nothing to stop or keep the child from repeating the same act.

A permissive parent will not intervene physically; instead, he leaves everything to chance and hopes that nothing bad happens to the kid. As a result, no limits are firmly set for such children. This is a not so good way to raise your child.

Good parenting is all about setting boundaries even though toddlers may not understand why you set the limits. A permissive parent does nothing to keep children from the pitfalls and hazards that lurk around. Though he may warn the child from a distance, no practical connection is built between parent and child.

Positive Parenting

Positive parents understand that children in their early years want to test boundaries. They are eager to experience something new in their own little way, so positive parents respond to their kids in a more emphatic way.

A positive parent would immediately attend to the child," I understand that you want to climb the couch, but it's not safe. So I won't let you."

Instead of yelling at the child, a positive parent calmly provides a distraction, "why not try to climb on the pillows instead?" At the same time, he gently removes the child and then directs him towards the distraction.

The aim of positive parenting is not only to guide the child but also to create lasting connections with your child. You cannot achieve that unless you explain to the child why he cannot do something he wants to do.

Positive parenting also requires that you set good examples for your kids to follow. Your kids are watching you, they will imitate you. How do you stop a toddler from screaming when you always yell in his presence?

Positive parenting may be the most demanding parenting style. It certainly requires giving ample attention to your kids, but it will instill good qualities in your child.

And those qualities will follow your child through life.

Positive Discipline

The literally meaning of discipline is to teach. From positive discipline, your kid learns self-control, and with that comes self-confidence and self-esteem. Positive discipline means that you show respect, you listen, you reward good behavior and you remind your child that you love her, whilst teaching her right from wrong.

On the other hand, negative discipline teaches the child fear, which leads to poor self-esteem.

Many child training issues fall into the category of discipline. Whether it is teaching your child to go to bed when he is supposed to, or teaching your child to share a toy, it's all about having a plan, setting limits and then following through with it.

Being a parent is not a popular job. You are not your child's buddy in a certain sense because being an effective parent sometimes means that your child will not like the decisions or rules you put in place in to guide and protect her. But that is okay, your child will still love you and even thank you many years later for helping her be the best person she can be.

If you let your toddler call the shots, you will be haunted as your child grows older and the stakes get higher. Today, it's demanding candy at the grocery store checkout line; tomorrow it's going to be partying with underage teens, drinking or drug use. Keep that in mind.

The 8 BEs of Effective Discipline.

1. ***Be a good role model***: Your kids are watching you and your actions speak louder than words.

2. **Be consistent** with whatever rule or limit you set.

3. **Be calm and brief**: The less you react, yell or lecture, the better. Make your comments short and sweet.

4. **Be quick**: Don't wait to discipline your child even when you are out in public. He won't remember why he is being disciplined if you wait till later.

5. **Be smart**: Decide which behaviors are serious enough to discipline and which ones to just ignore.

6. **Be realistic**: How much is your child really willing to endure you running errands or taking a phone call? Your kid needs attention. If you provide reasonable expectations, your child will act out less.

7. **Be positive**: Give your child positive attention, and recognize when he is good. Kids love positive attention, like hugs. But they will also accept negative attention like you screaming and yelling. So, if you praise your child for cleaning up his toys, you will see more of that

behavior. He won't have to resort to naughty behaviors to get you to notice him.

8. ***Finally, be a loving parent***: Remind your child that you love her. The behavior may be bad, but never tell a child that she is bad. After you are done disciplining her, say something nice and give her a hug. It shows that you are ready to move on and not dwell on the issue.

Remember, your child's behavior won't change immediately; you are planting the seeds of discipline right now, you need patience.

Positive Instructions for Toddlers

How do you speak positively to your toddler in spite of whatever the circumstances may be?

Always tell your child what you want, and stop talking about what you don't want. This is where most parents miss it.

Studies have shown that in the course of growing up, an average person from a relatively functional family was given nine to ten negative instructions for every positive instruction.

So their brains have been loaded with negatives, right from their toddler years and when they become parents, they also begin to talk to themselves and to their young kids like that.

Positive Instructions: How to Get Your Kids to Do What You Want Them to do.

An example of negative instruction is "don't touch the stove." When you say that to your toddler, the brain immediately creates a picture of what it heard, and the picture is 'touching the stove.' Even though your instruction was, 'don't touch the stove.' You have to give clear and positive instructions to your kids so as to produce the exact picture of what you want them to do in their brains.

If you say to the child "don't touch the stove" and the child touches the stove, you punish the child for touching the stove, and he suffers twice. First, he gets burned and second, he gets punished.

You need to say, "Keep your hand away from the stove! Avoid getting burned!" Now, that doesn't mean your child will never touch a hot stove.

If he touches it and gets burned, then your comment should be "let's put ice on it, next time keep your hands away from the stove! Avoid getting burned!"

Now, for situations that require dire urgency, a "Stop!" is okay. And then you tell the child what it is you want him to do.

When you say what you want to have done, your child's brain creates the picture, and he can obey. But when you give toddlers negative instructions, they may or may not change the picture. So when you say, "don't forget your homework" the picture their brain creates is 'forget your homework' and the kid forgets his homework and gets punished.

The preferable way of parenting is to say, "Remember your homework, and put it in your backpack now". By doing so, you're telling the brain exactly what you want and you are refraining from talking about what you don't want.

This is how you should instruct preschoolers and toddlers every time. Simple isn't it?

Learn to Give Positive Instructions

We talk to others the same way we talk to ourselves. A parent who continually gives negative instructions likely learned negative instructions while growing up.

We tend to do as we have been done to until we learn a different model.

Good news is it's easy to change that.

Start with yourself; tell yourself what you want yourself to do. Avoid talking about what you don't want yourself to do. Think about it, you want to stop yelling at your kids, so you keep telling yourself "don't yell at the kids," but you keep yelling.

When you say to yourself "don't yell at the kids," the picture your brain sees is you yelling at the kids, and your brain tends to follow whatever you put in working memory.

If you say to yourself "I speak kindly to my children, I tell my children what I want and avoid talking about what I don't want." You begin to see yourself speaking kindly to them and you will act accordingly.

You have to do this consistently. It doesn't mean that your child will almost immediately do whatever you tell them to do.

Nevertheless, research that shows that when you kindly, simply and directly give positive instructions to your kid, there is about an 85 percent chance that the child will follow what you've asked him to do.

Otherwise, you have got an 85 percent chance of them doing what you don't want them to do.

So give everybody an advantage by speaking kindly and telling your child what you want him to do instead of always talking about what you don't want them to do.

Limit Setting With Toddlers.

Toddlers are children in transition, which means that they are going from a state of infancy, where they are completely dependent on adults for everything they do, to a state of functional independence of a preschooler.

During this transition time, they are learning how to feed, walk, dress, and even use the bathroom independently. So this is a huge transition time.

Unfortunately, this can be a very trying time for parents, because during this time of transition, toddlers are trying to learn boundaries, so they may go from a very parent-pleasing child to someone who says 'no' a lot. They begin to test boundaries.

Ideally, that is what they should be doing at this stage in their growth; they are supposed to try and figure out what is expected of them.

Guidelines for Setting Limits with Toddlers

There are at least three things that work really well with setting limits for toddlers, they include; clarity, consistency, and kindness.

Clarity

Try to be clear with toddlers. This means to just give them a simple yes or no. In their earliest years, toddlers need little explanation. When they are four or five years old, and they ask why to everything, you can then begin to feed them with valid explanations for everything.

Toddlers just need the simple yes or no with little details. If they want the cookie before dinner, you can just say, "we don't have cookies before dinner, we have cookies after dinner." they don't need to know the nutritional facts of why they can't have cookies before they eat their fruits and vegetables.

Consistency

It is crucial to be consistent with toddlers especially when you set limits for them. You want those limits to sink into them. Every night when they ask for a cookie before dinner, you keep telling them "Not until after dinner! Not until after dinner!" Even if they ask you a hundred times, you are still going till have to say "Not until after dinner!" Consistency is what sets toddlers up to effectively learn what their boundaries are.

Kindness

It is important to be kind towards toddlers. You must have it at the back of your mind that they are passing through an inevitable phase in their development, and to be pushing boundaries as well as testing our limits is what they are supposed to be doing.

Even though they may drive you crazy sometimes, you have to demonstrate a good understanding of them. Tell your kid you understand he really wants that cookie, but he is going to have it only after dinner.

I hope that these guidelines can help you set limits with your toddler. When kids start to grow and enter into the phase where you really need to spell out for them what's appropriate and what's not, setting boundaries really helps.

Brain Development in the Early Years

When we talk about brain development, we mean the whole development of your toddler. This includes the physical, social and emotional arena.

Over the last few years, some discoveries have been made in the area of what is really happening in a child's brain and how their brains actually develop.

There are certain things you can do as a parent to assist your kid's development.

From the minute your baby is born, millions of connections begin to be established within their brains, which are responsible for creating the basis for their learning and growth.

Everything you do with your kid daily contributes to how these connections are formed. You don't need much time, effort or money to help your child's development.

The first five years are really important. But that doesn't mean you must get it right all the time. The idea is more about seeing those early years and exploiting them as a fantastic opportunity to get your kid off to a great start.

The Factors That Influence Your Child's Brain Development

Brain development research has shown that there are three main factors that influence your kid's brain development and their overall development. They include;

1. Genes,
2. Experiences, and

3. Relationships

Genes

Our lives begin with a genetic blueprint. We all inherit attitudes and behaviors from our parents. What happens when they are born is that two other incredibly important factors kick in. The first being our daily experiences and the second; relationships

Experiences

Toddlers go through daily experiences which lay foundations upon which their growth and development are built. Brains are built from the bottom up and growth happens from there. So everything you do with kids from the first day provides the platform for their future development.

Relationships

Kids thrive on strong and loving relationships which have the biggest impact on their brain development. Every time you love, care for or do anything for your children, you build that strong relationship which helps their development.

Simple Things You Can Do to Help Your Child's Development.

If you ask parents what they want for their children, this is what they all say, "we want our kids to be happy, healthy and to live a good life." And that is achievable.

I will touch on four areas you should look into in order to help your child develop. They may come to you as a confirmation of what you may already be doing or may be completely new to you, and you want to incorporate them.

These four areas are;

1. Care,
2. Learn,
3. Talk, and
4. Play

And as I mentioned earlier, they are not expensive. Kids do not need expensive toys or activities to help them achieve a healthy development.

How to Care For Your Toddler

Many parents see parenting in light of how they were raised. You may have often looked back at how you were raised and said to yourself, "I never want to raise my child like that." Other parents wonder how they can emulate their amazing dads or mums.

A lot of research has been carried out on parenting strategies, and one parenting strategy that actually stands out and makes a huge difference when it comes to children growth and development is to love your kids and show them you love them.

The best thing you can do for your child is to love him. To be love, warming and affectionate. I mentioned early on that there are three main factors that influence the growth and development of toddlers.

We saw that the relationships your children are exposed to from their earliest years have a lot of influence on their growth development.

The most prominent element in your relationship with your kids is to show them you love them. When you love them and express it, you are helping them build a strong foundation for their future learning and growth.

They can in turn and develop strong relationships with other people in their lives.

Create rituals: Rituals simply mean repeated things and activities that you do with your child. At bedtime, you can have a little bath ritual, read him a story, have a cuddle, and so on. You may also set up rituals for meal time. This gives kids a sense of safety, security, and confidence. It is a good thing to just share those lovely moments repeatedly with your toddler.

How Kids Learn

Parents are not required to always sit with their kids in order to teach them. What you need to do is get them involved in everyday life. Reading books, telling stories and singing songs, help to improve your child's literacy skills.

We don't think that children learn numerical skills at an early age, but they do. Activities like counting, measuring, simple comparisons, sorting mommy's clothes from daddy's clothes, telling the time, looking at the numbers on the letterboxes while walking around the neighborhood, all help your child to gain invaluable numerical skills.

And as I mentioned, you don't have to sit down with a tablet to teach them this stuff. These are stuff they can learn from everyday activities.

Play and Let Play

Toddlers do not need a lot of expensive toys to play. We live in a very screen-based world, and while we all use these devices, kids don't benefit a lot from screens, particularly in their early years.

They can learn so much more from playing with boxes, pots, and pans, things from the kitchen cupboards, playing outside, watching the ants crawl along the pavement and stuff like that.

Kids learn from exploring, trying things and experimenting. You have to give them the opportunity to run around, self-direct and follow their interests.

You don't need a lot of expensive things to make these happen. For kids, playing is not only fun, it's how they learn. Unfortunately, many parents have forgotten how to play, they are so busy working. But this is how kids learn and it's an important part if their development. Allow them to play, and play with them.

The other important thing is for them to play with others. As they grow older, they need to learn skills like sharing, negotiating and all other skills that they can only learn from playing with others.

You don't need to sit with them on the floor all the time. It is great if you can find the time to do that but it's also great to allow them to just roam around and play.

Talking to Your Toddler

Kids learn a lot from you when you just involve them in the conversation. To them, you may seem like the commentary on a documentary. But you can take time to talk to them also. Ask them questions even if they cannot talk. You can ask them their opinions. While shopping at the supermarket, you may say to your child, "oh, should we have pasta for dinner or should we just have this?"

The more you talk to your child the better. You may feel like you are talking to yourself, you are not. Toddlers listen and talking to them helps their growth and development.

So remember these four areas; care, being loving and affectionate, learning with them, talking to them as much as you can, and play. If you do nothing else with your child, just be loving and affectionate. And your child will be fine.

Showing them love and affection by involving them in your everyday life helps them develop a strong sense of identity and being part of a family. This helps their growth and development. Never forget that the first five years are more about giving your children a great start to life.

PART 2: MANAGING COMMON TODDLER BEHAVIOR

Finding the Causes of Toddler Behavior

What if your car refuses to start tomorrow morning? You may have to check a number of things. You may take a look at the battery and try to jump it. You may also check to see if you are out of gas. If the problem with your car is an empty gas tank, it will be a waste of time to jump the battery. In the same vein, filling up the gas tank will not solve the problem if the problem is in fact due to a flat battery.

An actual discovery what the real problem will save you the stress of applying unnecessary corrective measures.

This principle also applies to your child. When it comes to toddlers, misbehaving is only an effect. You have to find the cause. And by doing so, you can guide your child to behave right.

Toddlers misbehave in two major ways;

- *Failure to carry out your instructions, either ignorantly or otherwise.* For instance, you want her toys put away, and you give her a clear instruction, but she simply refuses.

- *Indulging in activities that you don't want.* Good examples include yelling, screaming, hitting, and other stuff.

Finding out the underlying cause of certain behaviors or misbehaviors exhibited by your toddler is not only crucial but simple.

Follow these simple suggestions:

Observe Your Toddler: You are familiar with your child and you know the one thing he does that you are not particularly happy with.

Watch out for this behavior, the next time it happens, observe what takes place before and right after. That way, you can draw out the behavioral pattern.

You may notice that your kid begins to throw her toys whenever her dad returns home. Try to see if there are other events that happen at this time.

She is probably looking for her father's attention or she's just hungry. She may also want her father to get down and play with her.

These are just simple examples that may shed light on the reason she behaves that way.

Asking your child one or two questions might help. "How are you feeling?" or "What happened?"

Notice that these questions do not probe into the "why." Asking toddlers the reason for their behavior is like you beating a dead horse. Toddlers cannot describe the reasons for the behaviors they manifest.

Even though kids may find it difficult to express what they are feeling at a point in time, they will more likely find words to describe what happened. This is how you can come to know what thrills her and what she considers important.

Involve other people: Consult other people in your child's life. They may have noticed this particular behavior or other behaviors that your child exhibit at certain times, which may even be hidden to you and you might be lucky to get a different perspective of the problem from these other people.

Getting to know the reasons for your child's behavior should be easy if you follow these suggestions.

And when you have found the reasons, you can then go on to what the solutions might be. The solutions in all cases should be tied to the reasons.

14 Causes of Toddler Behaviors

Below are some common reasons why toddlers misbehave. You will also find recommended solutions that you can proffer.

Make a note of these highlights.

Refer to them whenever an issue arises and see if the problem tallies with any item on the list.

Toddlers and the Rules You Set

Rules and principles are generally unknown or unclear to toddlers. Although they notice from the way you act and react that they are not permitted to do certain things, they still indulge.

Don't blame them because they are still unable to clearly understand the limits you set and their importance. If you have set lots of limits for your child, you need to reduce them and make them simple.

You also have to be consistent with the few rules you set for them, and communicate rules to them as clear as you can, and as many times as needed.

Toddlers may not always be receptive to changes that happen within the home. Maybe your child has just got a new sibling or you just relocated to another apartment.

Toddlers notice such changes, but they lack the ability to understand what has changed or to what degree and how they are required to learn and live by these new rules.

For the simple reason that they cannot adjust easily as grownups would, they will misbehave sometimes as they learn. You only need exercise patience with them.

Toddlers Are Curious Creatures

Many times, toddlers get into trouble for being curious. They want to discover what lies hidden in everything they come across. They also want to learn the consequences of their actions. And in doing so, they inevitably do things you don't want them to do or expose themselves to many dangers.

Curiosity is not bad in itself but it's got to be properly managed and you have a role to play as a parent.

Since your child won't stop trying to meddle in everything, you can reduce stuff around the home and get them your home in order.

This way you can cut back on her exposure to hazardous items around the house. If there is anything you don't want her to come in contact with, simply put it away from her reach.

Toddlers Want to Be Noticed

Grownups are not the only ones who want to be noticed, toddlers also crave for attention and it's only a proof of where we have come from when we show these traits as we grow.

When toddlers need your attention, it does not matter if rules are broken.

So they misbehave sometimes when it is, or when they think it is the only option available to get your attention. And it doesn't matter if you get angry, yell or smile. Any form of attention will suffice.

You can help your child cut back on misbehaving by giving her some attention before she asks for it.

Toddlers Want to Have a Say Too

We live in a world where adults call the shots, and that's only logical. But tell that to the kids. Everyone wants to have some control too, toddlers included. Kids want to express some authority whether they are conscious of that or not.

So when they do some things like hitting or screaming and you react, they feel some show of authority. At least they made you do something too. But it doesn't have to be that way; you can literarily give them some power.

I have mentioned this earlier, but it is worth mentioning again. If you find a subtle means to empower them, you can reduce the power struggle. You can achieve that by giving them choices within your permissible premise.

Place her coat and sweater before her, and let her make a choice. Such choices give them some impression that they also have some power and they don't need to yell or bite to show it.

Toddlers Are Who You Tell Them They Are

For some reason, if a child believes she is not right, she will keep doing wrong things. So keep telling him that he is good even when he does the wrong things. And if ever you let bad words slip out of your mouth once, make it up by telling him how good he is five times.

Toddlers Misbehave When They Are Sick or Tired

We all find it difficult to behave right when we are either weak or sick. Has it ever happened to you: you discipline your kid, only to discover later that she isn't feeling well?

Research has it that kids misbehave more at certain times of the day especially; 8 am, 8 pm and 6 pm. At these times, they are either stressed out or hungry.

You can address this issue by being proactive. Set out naptimes for your toddler and do not permit her to engage in any activity at this time.

Feed your child before she goes hungry and does not falter with any medical prescriptions she may have.

Toddlers Misbehave When They Are Frustrated

Kids frequently act up when they are attempting to accomplish something that's beyond their ability, without much success. After one or two trials, they get disappointed, scream, bite or even toss things. They may take it out on whoever is around them.

You can help your toddler in such situations. Talk to her and help her figure out how to get things done. You may also introduce her to kinds of stuff she can do.

Toddlers Have Their Own Interests

You may want your kid to do one thing but she is interested in something else. Kids also have their own ambition and it is only an indication that they are growing up.

What your child is doing at a point in time may seem more vital to her than what you want her to do. You have to find a middle ground and give some regard to her ambitions also because they mean a lot to her.

Parents ask for trouble when they try to get between toddlers and their ideas. Give your child at least ten minutes notice before sleep time, or any form of activity switch so she can be mentally prepared to stop whatever she is doing.

Endeavor to look at things from her perspective and maybe reason with her. Perhaps you need to accept her ideas sometimes. You may just find a solution that you will both be comfortable with.

Toddler Do What Kids Their Age Should Do

Sometimes, kids do things that are absolutely normal for their age group to do. Yet we see such actions as irregular. Sometimes, little children disagree with parents or guardians, they toss things. Often restless, they cannot seem to maintain one posture for a long time. And maybe they can't stop asking meaningless questions.

For kids their age, indiscipline is not often the issue. Therefore, discipline is not the solution. All they need is an environment that permits them to be who they are, toddlers. As a parent, you ought to identify what is normal for toddlers and draw limits for them that are in line with their age.

Try some tolerance. Because it is going to be a rather long ride till your child develops, and till then, she will continue to try something new all the time

Toddlers Actually Start Bad Habits

Most times, toddlers can't rationalize and they actually set out to do bad things without any thought. Such habits are not easy to curb because it's something that springs out of nowhere.

It's not as if your toddler planned to draw his clothes or stick his thumb in his mouth. They just do things like this without consideration and to them, nothing has changed.

Try to cut off the pattern. Give your kids something to keep their hands busy, to keep them from sucking their thumbs or drawing their clothes.

These are simple examples, there are many more bad habits that kids unconsciously begin, make them conscious of these habits.

Possibly you could give your kid a face each time she misbehaves in a particular way.

She should know that whenever she gets a face five times, she's in for a major disciplinary measure. Be creative; think about an approach to stop that behavior.

Toddlers Don't Know Other Ways to Get Around Situations

Sometimes, kids do the wrong things simply because they are unable to think about other ways get things they want.

Your child may want a toy that belongs to her playmate and what does she do? She hits the other kid or snatches the toy. Why does she do this? She hasn't yet developed the faculties to request the toy in a polite way.

But you can help her by teaching her how to connect and share.

Toddlers Are Just Who They Are

Some kids are simply full of energy and they are always seeking ways to release bits. Others are timid or just calm.

Some parents seek ways to influence energetic kids and get them to calm down while other parents attempt to get calm kids to be more active.

The truth is it is not possible to change some things. Children are born with some abilities that are peculiar to them and parents need to figure out how to make the most of their kids and whatever abilities they have and enjoy them for who they are.

Toddlers Emulate Others

If you don't want your kids doing something, keep them from being exposed to it. Kids learn a lot just by watching other people.

Likewise, what they see on TV or motion pictures stick with them and they try to do the same.

It is difficult for kids to keep from hitting when it's what they see in cartoons all the time. Your activities are an effective tool in instructing your toddler.

You can teach your toddler to eat vegetables by simply eating it in his presence. Same goes for all you don't want to have him do.

If you don't want your toddler copying someone or some kind of activity, keep him off, such people. And when he gets older, let him know who and what he should be imitating.

Toddlers misbehave when they are disappointed

When plans change and your kid's hopes get dashed, she may misbehave.

Adults communicate their feelings easily but it's not the case with toddlers; they find it hard to voice their feelings.

Ask your kid how she is feeling. Acknowledge her feelings and help her label what she feels with words.

Your child may misbehave for a whole lot of other reasons. Consider these suggestions and how they apply to your situation. It could be that your child gives you issues when it's time to go to bed, which is something many parents complain about.

If your toddler finds it difficult to stay in darkness all alone, you will continue to have this issue. Maybe it's not the darkness. Maybe it's the liquid she drank some minutes before bedtime, stress or just fatigue. You cannot approach these three different causes the same way.

You have got to partner up with your kid and find some way to relate to your child and other grownups.

Find the root cause of this behavior, and apply a viable solution when you find a clue. If it doesn't solve the problem, try another.

Frustrated Toddlers and How to Deal With Them

It is normal for our kids to be frustrated, though it can be inconvenient and very embarrassing. But frustration is just a normal human emotion. Squashing it all together isn't the solution.

The solution lies in showing your kids the way to cope, to deal with their frustrations, and express it in ways that are not hurtful to anyone else.

There is no tool that will magically make your kid never have this feeling again, the trick is just being able to distinguish when your kids are feeling frustrated, and they still have that little sense of reasoning and logical thinking, and those times when they are literally lost.

When to Apply Logic and Reasoning

You can tell when the door is still open for a logical approach and talking it out, and you can tell when it's no longer possible when reasoning and providing options don't actually help.

Talking is not always the answer, sometimes you just need to allow your kids the space to ride it out and then you can start using your tools of language and reasoning as well as engaging them after the storm has passed.

I know it's easier to deal with such situations when you're at home. But how do you handle it when you're in public? Simply carry your kid and take him out in a nice way. Then you can apply logic and tools.

If the door is still open and they are not yet in the full tantrum mode, the first thing you need to do is acknowledge their feeling, because sometimes parents tend to pretend like it's not happening, especially when they have an audience.

But quick statements like, "I know you are really frustrated, I knew you are really angry, I know it's not going the way you want it to go" sort of just normalizes their feelings.

The other thing it does is that it shows them the importance of working through the challenge. Whatever the challenge is, it's better to walk through to the other side rather than pretending it doesn't exist. This will be a lifelong lesson for your toddler. You have to teach your kids to face those tricky situations and those challenges.

So after you acknowledge it the next step is to give them some tools, so they can express themselves and settle down.

And this will depend on your time. Some kids like to run around, some kids like to physically get their frustration out by kicking or punching a pillow.

Some need to go and have a little yell in private. It could be anything. Anything that would make them experience that release and get better.

After they have that time to vent, then you can take the next step of helping them regain their calm.

Some ways to help them find their calm includes singing and mental distractions, like counting backward from ten. This will help them find their calm and come back to their center.

There are numerous strategies to calm toddlers down which are peculiar to each child. Find out what works for your child and make her smile again.

Biting Toddlers and How to Manage Them

Toddlers exhibit different forms of aggressive behaviors including hitting, screaming, and grabbing but none of them gets parents so concerned as much as biting does. This is definitely due to its primitive nature.

Parents have every reason to be concerned when their kids bite because biting is definitely one of the most dangerous aggressive acts they exhibit. And for these particular reasons, parents must find a way to address this behavior whenever it happens.

Toddlers below the age of two are fond of mouthing virtually everything they come across, and if you leave your fingers in their care, they might just innocently bite you.

However, when this act continues past the age of three, then you need to take them more seriously.

Like every other toddler behavior, biting in toddlers occurs as a result of several factors and if you will successfully manage this behavior in your child, you need to get a handle on why your child bites.

Why Toddlers Bite and What You Can Do About It

Toddlers normally want to get a better contact with things around them and to them, it seems to handle stuff is not enough, they have to feel their toys with their mouths.

Educate your child that biting people and animals around them is not allowed.

Keep objects small enough to be swallowed from their reach.

If the child's toy is big enough and cannot be swallowed, let him mouth that.

During the teething process, toddlers go through much pain and discomfort so it is common to see toddlers within this period rest their jaws on people's shoulders in order to pressurize their gums and alleviate some of the pain they feel. This is another reason they sometimes bite.

There are a couple of items you can provide to ease their sail through this period like teething biscuits and rings.

Also, without any sense of right and wrong, toddlers copy each other. When your child sees another child bite, he naturally wants to do the same, whether biting is right or wrong.

Sometimes, parents are tempted to slightly bite their children to show how painful it is to be bitten. This is a wrong approach. Never teach a child that it is wrong to bite by biting him.

Fourthly, toddlers bite when they sense danger. Asides throwing things and hitting, biting is about the only valid means of self-defense in their possession.

Help them develop a sense of safety wherever they are, especially within the home.

Toddlers bite for other reasons such as frustration, desire to be attended to, and inability to express themselves.

If your child happens to bite another kid, be calm, respond quickly, speak firmly to your child, let him know you won't tolerate that behavior, and draw his attention to the pain he's caused the person he bit.

Apply first aid to the victim and get your child involved in the exercise.

Toddler Aggression and How to Deal With It

Aggression is a common toddler behavior and it is also normal. I know it's annoying to say it's normal because we wish it wasn't so. We wish our kids never hit, kick or bite anyone but it is really normal because they are still learning to express their emotions.

And for a guy who has just turned two, he's just entering the phase of learning self-control and expressing his emotions in an acceptable way.

Toddlers are probably the most aggressive ones on the planet. They probably commit an act of violence something like every three minutes.

Sometimes we need to cut our kids some slack; not to the point of allowing them to hit or bite people anyway, but more in the sense of increasing empathy for what it is that they are going through at that point in time.

You can cut back on outings if you know they are really hurting and their response to pain is to act out or hit people.

Keys to Handle Aggressive Toddler Behavior

Be proactive

If you have been seeing your toddler behave a certain way for a while, you need to ask yourself, "What is the cause of this behavior? What is the common thread here? Is it toys? Is it a daytime nap? Is it hunger?"

Try to figure out what makes your kid aggressive and make adjustments, avoid them or even get rid of them completely.

You also need to consider the television shows or movies they are watching. Perhaps they are being exposed to aggressive contents.

A lot of kid shows on TV these days contain lots of fighting and violence, I mean superhero movies and the likes. Toddlers love them, but if your child is having a problem with aggressive behavior; it could as a result of what they are being visually exposed to.

Children do what they see even more than you realize. When they watch those kinds of movies, what they see is the punching and the kicking they do not really understand the plot behind those things.

They do not understand that Superman is doing the fighting to save or rescue. They just want to copy what they see, so be really careful with that.

Also, learn to respond quickly, especially where it is becoming a problem. Do not leave your kid alone to work it out all alone.

Move Away

Adopt zero tolerance for any kind of hitting or aggressive behavior. So your kid gets the message that he's welcome to play with his friends, but if he is not capable of playing safe, he will not be able to play with his friends.

The other thing about having a zero tolerance policy is to be predictable. Your kid must know what will happen if when he hits or kicks someone.

When they begin to hit and try to be aggressive, don't let them take you for a punching bag.

Don't let them think it's okay to punch mommy and have them continue to do that. So if you're sitting with them and they start giving you that attitude, get up and go sit on the couch and start doing your own activity.

By doing that, you are showing them the visual consequence of their actions. Next time, they won't want you to leave, and so they know they better not hit mommy, else she will leave.

Show That You Don't Like It

Don't just move away, let them see it on your face, and in your tone of voice that you don't like that. It is really important for kids to understand that their actions affect other people. They are very young and their brains are still developing. They still lack the empathy, but you need to show them because most of the time they don't know. They don't realize that their actions are hurting someone else.

Consequences are a part of life and they should be a part of your child's life as well. So if they have been hitting and you move away from them, then they begin to understand that it is a natural consequence that people leave when they do that.

Trust your instincts. If you are still feeling like something is not quite right, talk to your doctor because even if everyone always tells you it is normal, sometimes it is not. Just trust your gut because something could be going on that is causing this behavior that you just aren't aware of.

Anxious Toddlers and How to Manage Them

Having an anxious toddler is more difficult than having a typical toddler.

Toddlers are generally rough, but anxious toddlers are worse. They have more issues with eating than a typical toddler, they have a hard time with potty training because they are afraid, and they melt down all the time because they are so emotional. They are unable to control their feelings. So how do you parent them?

How to Help Toddlers Label Their Feelings

Toddlers have a hard time expressing their feelings.

Maybe you have so much confidence in your toddler's ability to express himself, but having an amazing vocabulary doesn't mean they have a good emotional vocabulary.

Toddlers don't know how to connect their feelings with words. And with an anxious kid, the sooner they can tell you how scared they are to do certain things, the better. So if you can teach them how to express their feelings, your life is going to be a lot quieter.

If they can't express their fear, say it for them, "oh dear, you are scared to go into the bath? The water seems scary? Don't worry; I will be there with you." Words like that will comfort them and prevent a meltdown. Doing that simple thing in various situations goes a long way in giving your kids an emotional vocabulary.

Teach them to Confront Their Fears

The second thing is to teach them early on to fight their fears. That doesn't mean you have to throw them at situations or force them to do things.

As an example, if your kid is afraid of a mask, go to the person that is putting it on and take it off (of course with an approval).

That is how to show your kid that it's just a guy underneath the mask. If he is afraid of shadows, turn the lights on and show him there is really nothing to shadows and they don't need to be scared.

Teaching them to figure out what their fears are all about is something they will take throughout their childhood and that is an amazing skill for them to have.

The last thing I want to add is that you should not be overly accommodating; otherwise, you will be helping your child's anxiety.

This applies to all ages. If your child is scared, do not over accommodate him, else you will exasperate the anxiety.

On the other hand, you shouldn't push your kid to the other end of the pool.

Find a middle ground.

Encourage your kid to go to the bathroom on his own, even if he was scared to do that.

Give him a reassurance that you will escort him to the doors (but he has to walk in by himself) and turn the light on.

Take them a little bit out of their comfort zone but you are actually getting into the water with them and letting them know it's safe instead of throwing them into the pool in their own.

PART 3:

HANDLING

TODDLER

TANTRUMS

What You Need To Know About Toddlers and Tantrums

Yes! Your child may have just turned two but you must do something to correct bad behaviors if there are any. Else, the 'terrible twos' as they are so often called will escalate to another 'terrible three' or 'awful four'.

The situation won't get any better if you don't adopt the skills for managing behaviors. You shouldn't just throw up your hands and hope your kid is going to outgrow bad behaviors. It may not phase out unless you do something about it.

Toddlers Love Choices

A two-year-old is just starting to discover his personality.

He is just beginning to understand that he has a will of his own. He wants to test that out, and see what he can do to get you to give him the things he needs from you. He is just trying to navigate the waters of what he can do, and what your role is as the parent. This basically is transition process for him.

One of the things most toddlers do around that is that they push boundaries. You have to remember that although they are pushing and testing you, they don't really have the power to make much difference.

Allowing some confined choice gives a toddler that feeling of having some control. But not so much that they become overwhelmed.

For instance, at story time, pick out two books and let your toddler select one of them. Set two pajamas or two pairs of socks before your child and let your toddler pick one.

Distraction Is a Tool

Another thing that is amazing about toddlers is how distractions work for them. For a toddler, frustration can quickly turn into a tantrum, but we can stop it before it starts, with some distractions.

For example, if you see your child getting frustrated with another child, as a parent, you can intervene and offer something else; you may pick up a different type of toy and try to entice your toddler with that instead of him hitting the other toddler for his toy.

If you are trying to wean a toddler, distractions are an excellent tool and a great way to steer them unto a different direction.

Sometimes, a behavior can actually go into a full-on tantrum, and that normally is just part of toddlerhood.

Toddlers are going to have tantrums occasionally, which basically is as a result of an overload of emotions; frustrations and anger at not getting what they want. These coupled with the limited skills they have to cope with these emotions. And so, being overwhelmed, they simply enter full tantrum mode.

If your child is upset with something he can't have or do at that moment, distract him with something else. You can use short clips of relaxing, calming and soft phonic songs. By the time the three-minute video is done, they usually forget what they were upset about and then you can move on together with them.

However, you have to draw the line between distracting them and bribing them.

Do Not Give In To a Tantrum

Now one thing you have to remember is that you can't give in to a tantrum under any circumstance. The minute you do that, you have just signed yourself on for years more of that exact same behavior. So you have to be careful, don't reward it.

Do not give in to manipulation of the tantrum by bribing your kid. It is really tempting, especially since it works most of the time, but don't. Remember, he may be a toddler today but you are essentially raising a future teen or even adult.

You want to make sure that your child learns the right way from early on because he is going to take that habit through life.

So you have to be careful about manipulating their acts; avoid things like giving candy to a child to stop him from crying.

When you do that, you are literally using chemicals to tell the brain that they can be rewarded anytime they cry. Kids are smart, and they do learn. So be careful what you teach them, intentionally or otherwise.

Do Not Ignore a Tantrum

At the same time, do not ignore it. Though, it's actually very difficult to ignore a tantrum, ensure you minimize your interaction.

There is really no point in trying to rationally speak to the child at this point. Just make sure they are safe, and clear the environment so they are not going to hit their heads on anything.

Do Not Punish a Tantrum

Punishing a tantrum will only add to the level of frustration. In fact, some kids cannot even hear you at that point.

You may talk to them till you are red in the face, get angry, or even put them in a time-out room, but they are really not going to hear or understand that. So just let it run its course.

Be Consistent

Use phrases like; Mommy says no! Mommy says no! There is a kind of security that toddlers get when they know what to expect.

If the rules don't change, and it's the same with mom and dad, they eventually stop acting. They learn to turn away from the tantrum and give up when they know mom isn't budging.

Sometimes they will stop the tantrum for a short while, and pick right back up. So what you can do is count to five in your mind, turn to them, and encourage them over (but don't go pick them just yet, you don't want them thinking they have the power). They will likely come over and calm down and forget about it.

As a parent, you have to know the difference between a fake and genuine cry. Sometimes, toddlers will work themselves up. They may start with a fake cry, and from there they get really upset. Some toddlers cannot calm themselves.

Let's say you have tried the distraction technique or every other strategy you know and you have been consistent, but they really have upset themselves, and they just won't yield, then it's your call as the parent to provide the comfort they need to help soothe them, because they are not able to do it on their own.

It's time for you to go over to them and give them a nice deep bear hug and some reassuring pats, and maybe some gentle rocking. Whisper some calming words into their ears which, for most kids will help them regroup and calm down.

Remember to reward them when they have either soothe themselves or allowed you to soothe them.

When the crying is done reward them. Let them know that you are fine with that and it is a good thing by giving special attention to them. You can say things like; good job! That's a happy girl! You make me happy!

Just spend a few moments to talk about how good it is that your child did stop the kicking or crying or biting, and how you really love that.

Toddler Tantrums: When to Be Concerned

Tantrums are normal for all toddlers, and they usually get better as they advance in years. Some children have a language delay, and tantrums are more intense in their case because they can't express their needs, and they are frustrated all the time. Nevertheless, as they increase in age and expression, their tantrums go down.

When are tantrums no longer normal?

Toddlers are adorable gems and usually soft-hearted. When a child throws 10 to 20 tantrums within a 30 day period, it is considered no longer normal.

It is not normal for your child to have frequent tantrums, as much as 5 in one day, and on multiple days.

So the frequency counts and you should be aware of that. Another pointer you should look out for is the duration.

It is not typical for a tantrum to last above 25 minutes on the average. Children should be developing self-regulatory skills and the ability to soothe themselves as they grow.

A child should be able to calm himself without having an adult intervene for him to stop.

It is also beyond the typical when your child consistently shows acts of aggression like hitting, kicking and biting during a tantrum. Also look out for some behaviors that seem out of place and unusual reactions to situations, like your child flapping his hands continuously and repetitively during a tantrum, or blinking over and over.

If the tantrum seems to be without cause and you cannot identify a trigger buzz or any recognizable reason, or maybe you can identify the reason but it's so minor that it shouldn't trigger a tantrum. Then you should be concerned.

The presence of these kinds of behaviors, intensity, and frequency of tantrums, may be a concern, especially if you are facing a lot of these things that I listed out, but they do not necessarily mean something is wrong with your toddler. It simply means you have to pay more attention to them than you normally would.

How to Handle Your Toddlers Temper Tantrum

Very often, toddlers roll on the floor to achieve their ends. This is a form of temper tantrums. They may want something in a shopping mall, and if you do not yield to their request, they will just sit there on the floor and start crying.

Some parents yield because they don't want to be seen as an unloving parent or they don't want to be embarrassed.

As a result, the child learns a certain behavior; that if he does that activity in a shopping mall, then he will get what he wants. That's the message that child gets.

Sometimes, kids demand an object which cannot be given to them, such as a knife or any other harmful object.

The child may cry for 5 to10 minutes, and even through the night. Some parents try to take their kid to another environment entirely as a means to distract so that the child forgets.

Other parents try to distract children by feeding them. What message does that send to the child? If I cannot get what I want, then I need to start eating. It's quite funny, but that is a message child carry through life as well.

Some parents yell when their kid refuses to listen to their explanations. This makes it even worse. The child's starts howling at an even higher pitch. And so the child will react in a totally different manner when a similar situation happens next time.

The child thinks, "Okay, I will cry, and what will mommy do? She will hit me, and I will cry even more for that. Let me see how long these people are able to manage my cry without intervening or giving me what I demand."

So how do you manage this whole issue?

Basically, if you feel that the child is asking for something reasonable, yield at the first request.

If you feel that whatever it is your child is asking for cannot be given, try to explain to him. If the child is adamant, then you stand your ground. Let him know you are not going to yield because it is in his best interest.

Gently inform the child that he is the first person that will be affected if you give that thing to them. What happens is that your child starts to believe that you have his concern as the priority. This is the communication pattern that you have to establish.

You must see to it that the child does not hurt himself in a major manner. So if they start banging their head, see to it that there is no sharp object nearby. Allow them to bang their head, it does not matter. After some time they will stop.

Initially, the child might cry for a while, but slowly they will understand that crying does not help. Slowly you will successfully train the child.

Conclusion

4 take home lessons

Here are the top four lessons you need to take to heart and apply to further help you understand to communicate with your Toddler

Behavior is driven by emotion, not logic

This is fundamental. The emotional state of a person no matter the age determines his behavior, and that includes your toddler. People act on their emotions and then they later justify their actions with logic. But small kids don't have the ability to use logic, so they act purely on emotion.

Say your child refuses to get dressed in the morning or eat his dinner. What is happening behind the scenes is that your child mentally connects the behavior you want to some kind of emotional pain. So no matter how many times you ask, your child won't cooperate.

Changing your child's emotional state is the key to getting the behaviors you want. Use specific language patterns that make it easy for your child to feel good about the behaviors that you do want. Once they feel good about it the behavioral change follows instantly.

Many parents try to use logic instead "If you eat that cookie you won't be hungry for dinner," or "if you don't wear this coat you'll be cold outside," or "you need to have a nap otherwise, you're going to be cranky this afternoon."

It simply doesn't work. I bet you can validate this by thinking back to your own experiences with your child. So make the necessary changes and see the desired results.

Quit overusing the word ' NO' when you talk to your kids.

You remember the story of a little shepherd boy was bored while watching the sheep, and so would cry wolf night after night to make the villagers come running? Well, before long they stopped responding to his false cries.

When a parent yells 'No' at every little thing, kids stop listening. People, including kids, are programmed to notice differences. If you're driving down the road, you don't notice the normal behavior of other cars or people walking on the sidewalk.

But if a car suddenly comes to a stop or a child suddenly runs into the street, you do take notice because something is different.

Ask yourself if you have said 'no' to your toddler so often that it has faded into the background, and become as ordinary as cars on the road or people on the sidewalk. The better alternative is to learn to manage your child's behavior without even having to resort to saying 'No' most of the time.

Build an Emotional Connection with Your Kid

If you want to have any chance of influencing your child's behavior, you must first build an emotional connection with your kid.

You notice that complete strangers get on with each other almost seamlessly by talking about the weather or gasoline prices. They unconsciously making general comments that they know the other person will agree with.

The agreement creates rapport. It's a natural process we all go through in adult relationships. It's as natural as breathing. But we often forget that we need to build rapport with our kids too.

If little Tracy is playing at the park, and you suddenly announce to her that it's time to go home. You have a huge chance of creating a fight because you missed the first step of building rapport. Creating this crucial emotional bridge will help you achieve your aim in handling the child's behavior.

Again, Use Positive Language

A language is a powerful tool and there are a bunch of tactics you need to learn to create the outcomes you want. Like I talked about before, use positive language instead of negative language. Ask your child to sit down instead of "stop jumping on the couch."

Ask him to hold his cup with two hands instead of "don't spill your milk." This is the opposite of how most of us speak.

But science has proven that speaking in negative terms and saying what you don't want will actually cause your child to do exactly what you're trying to avoid.

Young kids, unlike adults, don't have something called a critical faculty which helps to process the negatives in language.

It is vital that you imbibe positive communication strategies within your mind. It's not as hard as you might think, and the effects are fast and powerful.

Your life will become a lot more peaceful once you know how to fix, or even prevent most of those behavioral problems that you've been dealing with.

Talking positively to toddlers is your toddler toolbox. It's your security blanket for the terrible twos and beyond. It's what gives you the confidence you need to handle all those behavior problems.

Final Words from Joy Lamar

I am glad that you made it to the end of this piece and I am sure it meets your need.

Please spare some time to honestly review this book

Wish you a happy home with happy toddlers.

Thank you.

CPSIA information can be obtained
at www.ICGtesting.com
Printed in the USA
LVHW021446131118
596979LV00001B/71